William Henry Harrison

William Henry Harrison

Steven Otfinoski

AMERICA'S
9TH
PRESIDENT

Children's Press®
A Division of Scholastic Inc.
New York / Toronto / London / Auckland / Sydney
Mexico City / New Delhi / Hong Kong
Danbury, Connecticut

Library of Congress Cataloging-in-Publication Data

Otfinoski, Steven.
    William Henry Harrison / by Steven Otfinoski.
      p. cm. – (Encyclopedia of presidents)
    Summary: Details the childhood, military and political career, short presi-
dency, untimely death, and legacy of American's ninth president.
Included bibliographical references (p.) and index.
   ISBN 0-516-22761-0
   1. Harrison, William Henry, 1773–1841—Juvenile literature. 2. Presidents—
United States—Biography—Juvenile literature. [1. Harrison, William Henry,
1773–1841. 2. Presidents.] I. Title. II. Series.
E392.O84 2003
973.8'6'092—dc21

                                    2002005897

CHILDREN'S PRESS and associated logos are trademarks and or registered
trademarks of Scholastic Library Publishing. SCHOLASTIC and associated
logos are trademarks and or registered trademarks of Scholastic Inc.
1 2 3 4 5 6 7 8 9 10 R 12 11 10 09 08 07 06 05 04 03

Contents

Chapter 1

A Distinguished Family

William Henry Harrison had the pedigree of a president. His family was among the most distinguished in Virginia. He seemed destined for a life of service and great accomplishment. He excelled as a soldier, territorial governor, and Washington politician, but his road to the presidency was a long and winding one. The great honor came late in his life—as it turned out, a little too late.

Harrison was born on February 9, 1773, at Berkeley, the family plantation on the James River in Charles City County in eastern Virginia, the son of Benjamin and Elizabeth Bassett Harrison. William Henry's father was the fifth in a line of Benjamin Harrisons stretching back to the earliest days of the colony. The first Benjamin Harrison arrived in America from England in 1632 and settled in Jamestown, the first permanent English settlement in America. He played a significant role in the colony's government, assisting the governor. His son, Benjamin II, was a soldier and helped found Virginia's first institute of higher learning, the College of William and Mary, in 1693. Benjamin III, William's great-grandfather, served the colony as attorney general and treasurer. His grandfather, Benjamin IV, was a member of the House of Burgesses, Virginia's legislative body. William's father, Benjamin Harrison V, was one of the most distinguished members of the family. He served in the Continental Congress before and during the American Revolution and was one of the 56 signers of the Declaration of Independence. When William Henry was a small boy, his father served as one of the first governors of the new state of Virginia, part of the independent United States. William's mother, Elizabeth Bassett, also came from an old and distinguished family.

William Henry was the youngest of seven children. Virginia had few schools and like other well-to-do families, the Harrisons hired tutors to teach their children at home. William studied Latin, Greek, literature, history, and arithmetic, and a smattering of geography and astronomy. He enjoyed his subjects but did not excel in any of them. "All during my youth," he once wrote a friend, "my father admonished me about my studies."

As a Harrison, great things were expected of him, yet through most of his youth he showed few signs of greatness. When he was 14, his father sent him to

William Henry Harrison was born in 1773 in this house in eastern Virginia, near the colonial capital, Williamsburg. It was built by his grandfather and his father.

Hampden-Sydney College in Prince Edward County, Virginia. He was there only a short time when his father pulled him out of the school because he was unhappy with the religious instruction. While at Hampden-Sydney, however, William developed a deep love of Greek and Latin literature and would remain a devoted reader all his life.

William was apprenticed to a doctor in Richmond, Virginia. Perhaps he chose to study to become a doctor, or perhaps his father decided for him. In Richmond, he lived with his older brother Benjamin. In 1790, he enrolled in the Medical School of Pennsylvania in Philadelphia, where he studied under Dr. Benjamin Rush, the most famous physician in the young nation. Just when it seemed William would become a medical doctor, fate intervened. On April 25, 1791, his father died suddenly. William was placed under the care of a guardian, the well-known Philadelphia financier Robert Morris. Soon afterward, William made an announcement that shocked both his guardian and his mother. He wanted to leave school and volunteer for the army.

Since the end of the Revolutionary War, the small U.S. Army was used mostly for protecting the settlers heading to western territories from hostile Native Americans. The frontier outposts where soldiers lived were crude, and life there was boring, except when the Indians attacked.

Dr. Benjamin Rush

Dr. Benjamin Rush (1745–1813), with whom Harrison studied briefly, was one of the great figures in the early history of the United States. He graduated from the College of New Jersey at 14, and studied medicine in Philadelphia, Great Britain, and France. In 1769, at the age of 23, he was appointed the first professor of chemistry in colonial America at the College of Philadelphia (later the University of Pennsylvania).

Rush was a strong supporter of colonial independence and was a signer of the Declaration of Independence. He became a lifelong friend of John Adams and Thomas Jefferson. During the Revolutionary War, he served as surgeon-general of the patriot army in the middle colonies. After independence, Rush helped establish the finest medical school in the United States. He organized a clinic for the poor in Philadelphia, and took special interest in treatment of the mentally ill. He was a pioneering crusader for the abolition of slavery and for increasing educational opportunities for women.

☆ ★ ☆

To the Northwest Territory

Harrison's guardian, Robert Morris, tried to talk him out of joining the army, urging him to continue studying medicine or to go into government service, as so many in his family had done. Harrison was young and adventurous, however, and saw his future in the army. Through family connections, he gained an interview with President George Washington. Washington, the commander in chief of the patriot army in the Revolutionary War, had been a friend of Harrison's father and

The Northwest Territory

The region known as the Northwest Territory consisted of the present-day states of Ohio, Indiana, Illinois, Michigan, Wisconsin, and parts of Minnesota. It was a vast wilderness, home to many Native American tribes, which had been first explored by French traders in the 1600s and early 1700s. In 1763, at the end of the French and Indian War, the British took over the region, and settlers from the American colonies began to move in. During the Revolutionary War, the settlers found themselves in a deadly struggle against the British and their Indian allies.

In the Treaty of Paris in 1783, Great Britain recognized the claims of the United States to lands bordered by the Ohio River on the south, the Great Lakes on the north, and the Mississippi River on the west. Four years later, Congress passed the Ordinance of 1787, establishing this huge region as the Northwest Territory. The ordinance set out plans for surveying and organizing the territory, and it outlined the way in which the region could be broken up into smaller units that could be admitted as states when they reached a minimum population of 60,000.

British trappers and traders remained in the region and opposed American expansion. They stayed in touch with British military authorities in nearby Canada and formed alliances with Native American tribes against the settlers. During the 1790s, the U.S. Army was dispatched to the territory to protect the settlers and to keep the Native Americans at bay. Young William Henry Harrison would be a participant in their crucial battles.

☆ ☆ ☆

Facing page:
This early map shows the old Northwest, where Harrison served as a soldier and government official. The Mississippi River is at the left, the Ohio River runs along the bottom, and the Great Lakes are at the top.

A MAP of the north west parts of the UNITED STATES of AMERICA
The several divisions on the NW of the Ohio is the form which that Country is to be laid off into States according to an ordinance of Congress of may the 20th 1785
The author presents this to the public as the production of his leisure hours and flatters himself that altho it is not perfect few capital errors will be found in it He has not attempted to take the exact meanders of the Waters but only their general course — In forming this Map he acknowledges himself to have been indebted to the ingenious labours of Thomas Hutchins and Willm. McMurray Esqrs But from his own Surveys and observations he was led to hope he could make considerable improvements on those and all that have gone before him. How far he has Succeeded is now Submited to the impartial public by their very hble servt — John Fitch
To Thos. Hutchins Esqr Geographer to the United States
SCALE of MILES
LAKE SUPERIOR
Ile Royal
Philipeaux I
The line between the UNITED STATES of AMERICA and Canada According to the Definitive Peace Signed at Paris Septr 3d 1783
LAKE HURON
LAKE MICHIGAN
LAKE ERIE
An High Plain
Lake of the Woods
Falls of St. Anthony
Winnebago
Detroit
Niagara Falls
Ft. Erie
ILLINOIS RIVER
Wabash River
OHIO RIVER
MISSISSIPPI RIVER
Green R.
Lexington
PART OF THE KENTUCKEY COUNTRY
Fort Pitt
PART OF PENSYLVANIA

was happy to give the young man an officer's commission and an assignment to the Northwest Territory.

After several weeks of training, Ensign Harrison was ordered to march 80 recruits to Fort Pitt, in present-day Pittsburgh, Pennsylvania. They reached the fort in 21 days. Fort Pitt was a rough and filthy place, and at first Harrison found the rugged frontiersmen rough and undisciplined. In time he came to appreciate them as men and as able soldiers. Among the other young officers he met were future explorers Meriwether Lewis and William Clark. Another was Solomon Van Rensselaer, who became one of Harrison's lifelong friends.

Soon Harrison and his men were sent down the Ohio River in flatboats to Fort Washington. The settlement around the fort later became the city of Cincinnati, Ohio. A short time before their arrival, Fort Washington had been attacked by the Shawnee and Miami Indians. Some six hundred soldiers had been killed and the fort's commander, General Arthur St. Clair, had been wounded. To secure the fort and launch an aggressive campaign against the Indians, President Washington sent General "Mad Anthony" Wayne to take charge of all forces in the territory. Wayne was one of the heroes of the Revolution and just the man for the job. He arrived at Fort Washington in the spring of 1792.

"Mad Anthony" Wayne (1745–1796)

Anthony Wayne's reputation for reckless bravery in battle earned him his unusual nickname. He became one of the most successful and admired generals in the Revolutionary War. When the Revolution broke out in 1775, he raised his own regiment in Pennsylvania and first fought in an unsuccessful invasion of Canada. Within two years his achievements earned him the rank of brigadier general. He fought bravely at the battles of Brandywine Creek and Germantown near Philadelphia, and in 1779, he captured a British-held fort at Stony Point, New York, in a daring action requiring his men to wade through waist-high water. Late in the war, he helped drive the last British troops from Georgia.

When President Washington recalled Wayne to duty in the Northwest in 1792, he had been retired from the army for nearly nine years. He soon showed that he had lost none of his daring or skill.

☆ ★ ☆

The Battle of Fallen Timbers

At Fort Washington, General Wayne was especially impressed with junior officer William Henry Harrison. Many officers dealt with the tedium of frontier life by getting drunk and fighting with fellow officers. Harrison preferred to sit alone with a good book. He was also a keen student of the military situation. Harrison suggested that two new forts be built along the border of present-day Ohio and Indiana to better secure the territory. Wayne agreed and put Harrison in charge of

"Mad Anthony" Wayne was a Revolutionary War hero whose bravery sometimes seemed wildly reckless. He took command of forces in the Northwest Territory in 1792, and Harrison fought under him at the Battle of Fallen Timbers in 1794.

the construction. He also promoted him to lieutenant and made him an *aide-de-camp*, or confidential assistant.

By May 1794, both Fort Greenville and Fort Recovery were finished. A third, Fort Defiance, was built that summer. The Shawnees and Miamis, under the leadership of their chiefs Little Turtle and Tecumseh, were preparing for another assault. Wayne took the initiative and marched 3,000 troops north to the British Fort Miami, near present-day Toledo, Ohio. Lieutenant Harrison, who had provided the battle plan, accompanied him. As the Americans approached the fort, the Shawnees and their British allies hid behind uprooted trees and fired on them. The Battle of Fallen Timbers had begun. Vastly outnumbered, the Indians were quickly driven back. They tried to gain entry into Fort Miami, but the British, who did not wish to get into a more serious fight with the Americans, kept them out. Wayne, in his turn, did not want to start a war with the British, so he did not attack the fort.

The battle was a decisive victory for the Americans. Wayne had lost only 33 men; the Indian and British casualties were close to 500. As Wayne's aide-de-camp, Harrison had carried his orders on horseback across the battlefield in the thick of the fighting. In his report of the battle, General Wayne praised Harrison and another officer for having "rendered the most essential service by their conduct and bravery exciting the troops to press for victory." Another officer went

American troops charge Shawnee warriors at the Battle of Fallen Timbers in 1794.

even further and claimed that if Harrison "continue[s] a military man, he will be 'a second Washington.'"

Wayne and his army traveled back to Fort Washington. As for the Indians, they were beaten, but not vanquished. There would be other critical battles in the region, and Harrison would play a leading role in them.

Chapter 2

The Treaty of Greenville ——————————

Determined to settle his difference with the Indians peacefully, General Wayne invited the tribal chiefs to a meeting in August 1795 at Fort Greenville. The 92 chiefs who attended agreed to give up their lands and lay down their weapons. In return, Wayne gave them $20,000 in goods and provided them with about half again as much over several more years. The Treaty of Greenville, signed on August 3, gave the United States a large portion of present-day Ohio. Harrison, who was present, was one of the 27 white men who signed the treaty.

A young Shawnee warrior named Tecumseh stayed away from the meeting and soon condemned the other chiefs for signing away lands that belonged to all Native Americans. Tecumseh moved west with his Shawnees into present-day Indiana, but he called for all other tribes not to sell their homelands to the whites. He was becoming the leader of Native Americans resisting the United States.

Courtship and Marriage

In the meantime, Harrison had found a new interest at Fort Washington. In 1794, he met Anna Symmes, the attractive 20-year-old daughter of a wealthy landowner and judge. Miss Symmes had recently moved with her family to North Bend, about 16 miles (26 kilometers) from the fort. Harrison and Anna began courting, but it was soon clear that Anna's father did not approve of a soldier for a son-in-law. He reportedly said of Harrison, "He can't bleed [be a doctor], plead [be a lawyer], nor preach [be a clergyman], and if he could plow [be a farmer], I should be satisfied."

On November 25, 1795, when Judge Symmes was away on business, Harrison and Anna eloped and were married. Symmes was furious. He asked Harrison how he planned to support his new wife. "My sword is my means of support, sir!" replied the soldier boldly. Symmes was impressed with his son-in-law's confidence and in time they became good friends.

John Symmes soon had good reason to be proud of his new son-in-law. Harrison was promoted to captain and made temporary commandant of Fort Washington. He proved to be an effective and thorough administrator. In 1798,

Anna Symmes Harrison had many qualities that would make her an excellent first lady. She was born in Flatbrook, New Jersey, on July 25, 1775. Her father, John Cleves Symmes, was a military leader in the American Revolution and served in the Continental Congress after the war's end. He was an important landowner and judge in the Northwest Territory. It took great courage for Anna to go against his wishes and marry William Henry Harrison. She demonstrated the same strong spirit in giving birth and raising and educating ten children while her husband was often away on military or political business.

Anna Harrison eloped with William Henry Harrison when her father would not agree to their marriage. She is shown here at about the time Harrison was elected president.

Mrs. Harrison was a warm and gracious hostess at the Harrison homes in the Indiana Territory and later back in North Bend. Their door was open to passing visitors, who were often welcomed to stay the night. During her long life she endured many tragedies. Her husband and all but two of her children died before she did. In 1858, when she was in her 80s, her home burned to the ground. She died at age 88 on February 25, 1864.

☆ ★ ☆

President John Adams, who succeeded Washington in office, appointed Harrison secretary of the Northwest Territory. Harrison resigned from the army and built a house in North Bend for his wife and their growing family.

Part of Harrison's job as territorial secretary was to keep the capital informed on affairs in the territory. The following year, he was elected territorial delegate to the U.S. Congress. In his short time in Washington, Harrison helped push through an important piece of legislation that would bring many more people into the Northwest Territory. Until then, the government sold land in parcels of 640 acres (one square mile, or about 260 hectares). Harrison argued that only wealthy investors could afford to buy such large parcels. The new law, called the Harrison Land Law, reduced the size of land parcels from 640 to 320 acres (130 hectares), allowing ordinary Americans to buy land to settle on.

Territorial Governor

In 1800, the Northwest Territory was divided into two parts. The eastern part, consisting of present-day Ohio and eastern Michigan, kept the name Northwest Territory. The western part was called the Indiana Territory. It included not only present-day Indiana, but also western Michigan, Illinois, Wisconsin, and southeastern Minnesota. President Adams appointed Harrison the first governor of the Indiana Territory.

In January 1801, Harrison and his family moved to the tiny territorial capital of Vincennes, on the Wabash River, along the present-day border between Indiana and Illinois. He built a brick mansion that he modeled after Berkeley, his childhood home in Virginia. It was named Grouseland in honor of the grouses, large pheasantlike birds that roosted on the property. It would become a welcoming stop for any traveler passing through.

As the new governor, Harrison had many duties. He appointed judges, officials, and military officers. He helped divide the vast territory into smaller units of counties and townships. He commanded the militia and adopted laws. His hardest task was dealing with Native Americans. Having once fought them, Harrison now found himself in the position of defending their rights. This wasn't easy. The white settlers pouring into the territory treated the Indians cruelly. "[The chiefs] say their people have been killed," Harrison wrote to Secretary of War Henry Dearborn, "their lands settled on—their game wantonly destroyed—their young men made drunk and cheated. . . . Of the truth of these charges, I am well convinced." To his credit, he did what he could to help. He tried to prosecute whites who murdered Native Americans, banned the sale of alcohol to them, and had them inoculated for smallpox, a deadly disease that took many lives.

At the same time, Harrison had orders from the federal government to conclude treaties for Native American land to meet the demand from new settlers

Grouseland, the home the Harrisons built in Vincennes, the capital of the Indiana Territory.

who continued to pour into the territory. Many Native American tribes signed treaties, giving up their lands in return for money, then moved farther west. By 1809, treaties had given the U.S. government nearly all of present-day Illinois and Indiana.

Not all Native Americans were willing to move on, however, and their resentment was growing. They found a leader in Tecumseh and his brother, Tenskawatawa, who was known as "the Prophet." Tecumseh was the political and military leader of the resisting tribes, and the Prophet was their spiritual leader. Both men were eloquent orators. Tecumseh's goal was to unite many different tribes to fight the whites and drive them from their lands. It was a bold idea that no other Indian leader had attempted on such a scale.

In September 1809, Harrison negotiated the Treaty of Fort Wayne, his most ambitious peace treaty yet. The chiefs of the Miami, Potawatomi, and Delaware tribes sold about 3 million acres (about 4,700 square miles) of land on the Wabash and White Rivers to the government. When Tecumseh heard about the treaty, he was furious.

Harrison knew he had to deal with Tecumseh quickly in order to avoid more bloodshed. He invited the Shawnee chief to Vincennes to meet with him to discuss their differences. Tecumseh accepted and arrived at Grouseland in August 1810 with many warriors. The situation was tense, but Harrison kept a cool head.

Tecumseh (1768-1813)

Generally acknowledged as one of the greatest of Native American leaders, Tecumseh's name in his native Shawnee means "shooting star." Like a shooting star, he lit up the sky of American history for a brief moment before falling in defeat.

Tecumseh was born near present-day Dayton, Ohio, in 1768. His father, a Shawnee chief, was killed along with two of Tecumseh's brothers fighting against the early settlers. Tecumseh grew up to continue the struggle to drive the whites from their homelands, and he came up with a plan to do so. He realized that the Indians were doomed to defeat unless they could unite in their struggle. A great orator as well as a great warrior and leader, Tecumseh was just the person to organize and lead such an alliance. For years he traveled tirelessly across the west and south, talking to different tribes and winning their support.

His dream of a united Native American opposition to the United States fell apart in 1811 after the Battle of Tippecanoe. Soon after, Tecumseh joined the British in the War of 1812 against the Americans and died in 1813 at the Battle of the Thames River. "A more gallant warrior does not . . . exist," said British general Isaac Brock.

Perhaps the best tribute to Tecumseh came from his longtime rival, Harrison. "If it were not for the vicinity of the United States," Harrison said, "he would perhaps be the founder of an empire that could rival in glory Mexico or Peru."

☆ ☆ ☆

Tecumseh, the gifted leader of the Shawnee people, who tried to unify Native Americans to fight against American settlers. He formed an alliance with the British in Canada and is shown wearing a British military uniform.

When he offered Tecumseh a chair to sit in, the chief refused. "The Earth is my mother and on her bosom I will recline," he replied. Both men took each other's measure and were impressed. But Tecumseh would not be talked into a peace treaty by Harrison. When the meeting ended, no progress had been made. Harrison and Tecumseh met twice more the next year, but to no avail. When their last meeting broke up, Harrison was certain that the next time they met it would be on the battlefield.

The Battle of Tippecanoe

Harrison knew that to win, he would have to strike first. Tecumseh was away to organize tribes in the south. During his absence, Harrison led nearly a thousand men against Prophetstown, a village established by the Prophet at the mouth of the Tippecanoe River, 150 miles (240 km) north of Vincennes.

The army arrived near the Indian stronghold late on November 6, 1811. Harrison decided to make camp for the night and attack the following morning. An hour before dawn, the soldiers were awakened by war whoops and firing. The Indians were attacking. The soldiers quickly rallied. After several hours of desperate fighting, the Indians were driven back and disappeared into a nearby marsh. Harrison advanced and burned Prophetstown to the ground.

Harrison led his troops to the Tippecanoe River near present-day Lafayette, Indiana, in 1811. The Shawnee attacked at dawn, but Harrison counterattacked. He finally drove the Shawnee back and captured their settlement, called Prophetstown.

Harrison reported that he had achieved a great victory over the Indians that day. Later historians are not so sure. Some say that Tippecanoe was a major blow to Tecumseh's plans of Indian unity, but others claim the battle did little to stop Indian aggression in the region. At the time, however, the battle was seen as a great victory for the United States, and Harrison soon gained the nickname "Old Tippecanoe." Nearly 30 years later, the event would play a critical role in his bid for the presidency.

Tecumseh promised to avenge the Americans' victory. His opportunity came eight months later. In June 1812, the United States and Britain went to war. Tecumseh, who had already received assistance from the British, offered his services to the British in the War of 1812 and was warmly welcomed.

Hero of the War of 1812

Beginning in 1811, relations between Great Britain and the United States were strained to the breaking point. A group of young congressmen known as the War Hawks demanded that the United States challenge the British. On the seas, British navy ships were stopping and searching U.S. ships and *impressing* sailors—carrying them off to work in the British navy against their will. In the Northwest, the British still maintained forts and were providing encouragement and supplies to Native Americans who were attacking U.S. settlements.

Finally, President Madison asked Congress for a resolution of war against Great Britain, and it passed on June 18, 1812. For the first time in 30 years, the nation was at war with a major world power. Things went badly for the United States in the early weeks of the war. British forces captured Fort Dearborn (now Chicago), and U.S. general William Hull surrendered the trading post of Detroit.

President Madison recalled William Henry Harrison to active army duty and appointed him commander of the armies in the Northwest with the rank of brigadier general. Harrison resigned as governor of the Indiana Territory and took military command.

In 1813, the U.S. Navy scored a major victory against a British fleet in

Fast Facts

THE WAR OF 1812

Who: The United States against Great Britain

When: The U.S. declared war in June 1812. The war was ended by the Treaty of Ghent, signed in December 1814, but fighting continued into January 1815.

Why: Britain was restricting U.S. shipping, seizing cargoes and sailors from U.S. ships. It was also interfering with settlement in U.S. western territories and providing help to Native Americans who were attacking American settlers.

Where: In the United States, Canada, and on the Atlantic Ocean. The United States organized several unsuccessful invasions of Canada while surrendering forts in the Northwest. In 1813, the U.S. Navy defeated a British fleet in Lake Erie, leading to land victories at Detroit and at the Thames River (in nearby Ontario). In 1814, the British captured Washington, D.C., and burned public buildings, but were defeated soon afterward in Baltimore. British troops threatened New Orleans but were driven off in January 1815 by a force led by Andrew Jackson.

Outcome: In the Treaty of Ghent, both sides agreed to boundaries set up before the war. Britain agreed to end impressment of American seamen and give up British forts south of the Great Lakes. The treaty also settled disputes about fishing rights and commercial relations.

the Battle of Lake Erie, weakening the British hold on Detroit. Harrison took advantage of the situation. With a force of 3,000, he attacked and recaptured the settlement. Then he pursued the British across the border into Canada. On October 5, 1813, a week after his victory at Detroit, he confronted a combined force of British and Native American soldiers, including his old rival Tecumseh, at the Thames River. Harrison drove the British force off the field, scoring a decisive victory for the Americans. The battle ended the British threat in the Northwest. It also ended Tecumseh's dream of a united Indian resistance to the United States. The noble chief was killed in the fighting.

On other fronts, the war was still a seesaw struggle. In the summer of 1814, the British captured Washington, D.C., and burned the Capitol and the Executive Mansion. Weeks later, however, the Americans won important victories at Baltimore and on the shores of Lake Champlain near Plattsburgh, New York. Meanwhile, British and American diplomats were discussing an end to the war in Ghent, a city in present-day Belgium. Finally, they agreed on terms for ending the fighting and signed the Treaty of Ghent on December 24.

As news of the treaty was on its way to the United States, a British fleet landed near New Orleans, threatening the city at the mouth of the Mississippi River. Andrew Jackson of Tennessee assembled a force on land and sea to defend the city. On January 8, Jackson won a stunning victory, driving the British back

In 1813, Harrison recaptured Detroit from British forces, then chased them into Canada. At the Thames River there, he achieved his greatest victory. The Shawnee chief Tecumseh was killed in the battle.

Evening Gazette Office,

Boston, Monday, 10, a.m.

The following most highly important handbill has just been issued from the Centinel press. We deem it a duty that we owe our Friends and the Public to assist in the prompt spread of the Glorious News.

Treaty of PEACE signed and arrived.

Centinel Office. Feb. 15, 1815, 8 o'clock in the morning.

WE have this instant received in Thirty-two hours from New-York the following

Great and Happy News!

FOR THE PUBLIC.

To BENJAMIN RUSSELL, *Esq. Centinel-Office, Boston.*

New-York, Feb. 11, 1815—Saturday Evening, 10 o'clock.

SIR—

I HASTEN to acquaint you, for the information of the Public, of the arrival here this afternoon of H. Br. M. sloop of war *Favorite*, in which has come passenger Mr. CARROLL, American Messenger, having in his possession

A Treaty of Peace

Between this Country and Great Britain, signed on the 26th December last.

Mr. Baker also is on board, as Agent for the British Government, the same who was formerly Charge des Affairs here.

Mr. Carroll reached town at eight o'clock this evening. He shewed to a friend of mine, who is acquainted with him, the pacquet containing the *Treaty*, and a London newspaper of the last date of December, announcing the signing of the Treaty.

It depends, however, as my friend observed, upon the act of the President to suspend hostilities on this side.

The gentleman left London the 2d Jan. The Transit had sailed previously from a port on the Continent.

This city is in a perfect uproar of joy, shouts, illuminations, &c. &c.

I have undertaken to send you this by Express—the rider engaging to deliver it by Eight o'clock on Monday morning. The expense will be 225 dollars.—If you can collect so much to indemnify me I will thank you to do so.

I am with respect, Sir, your obedient servant,

JONATHAN GOODHUE.

We most heartily felicitate our Country on this auspicious news, which may be relied on as wholly authentic—Centinel.

PEACE EXTRA.

A handbill announces to the people of Boston that the War of 1812 is over. The Treaty of Ghent was signed in December, but the news did not reach Boston until February 13!

and ending their offensive. Jackson became a national hero, and the glory of his victory would help him gain election as president in 1828.

Meanwhile, Harrison had resigned his army commission in May 1814, well before the war ended. He had been quarreling with Secretary of War John Armstrong, and he had family business to attend to. His family had moved back to North Bend, now in the state of Ohio, and his father-in-law had died. No longer territorial governor and no longer an army officer, he was once again a private citizen.

At 41 years of age, he had much to be proud of. In his twelve years as governor of the Indiana Territory, he had presided over the development of that vast territory. Only two years later, the part of the region he knew best was admitted to the Union as the state of Indiana, with a population of 64,000 people. At the same time, Harrison had gained success as a military commander, scoring victories over the Shawnee at Tippecanoe in 1811, and against the British at Detroit and Thames River in 1813.

In North Bend, Harrison planned and supervised the building of a fine new home for his wife and children. He planned to settle down and become a gentleman farmer, but soon he would return to public life.

Congressman and Senator ——————

In 1816, after two years in North Bend, Harrison ran for a seat in the

U.S. House of Representatives and easily won. He entered politics

partly to clear his name. His quarrel with Secretary of War Armstrong

in 1814 involved charges that he had made a personal profit from sell-

ing army supplies. He was never charged with official wrongdoing,

but the accusations continued to reappear. Once in Washington,

Harrison asked that the accusations be investigated by a House com-

mittee. The committee found no evidence against him and all charges

were dropped.

In his two years in the House, Harrison initiated two worth-

while pieces of legislation. Recognizing how ill-prepared the military

was for the War of 1812, he introduced a *bill* (a draft for a new law)

that would require universal military training for all young men. This was an idea far ahead of its time, and it did not become law. The U.S. Army was still poorly prepared 45 years later, when the Civil War began. Harrison's second bill was more practical. It called for payment of public funds to soldiers wounded in the recent war and to families of soldiers who had been killed. The bill passed.

Harrison made one political misstep during his service as a representative. When General Andrew Jackson invaded Florida (then a possession of Spain) and captured two Spanish forts, Harrison was one of the congressmen who wanted to censure Jackson. No censure was ever passed, but Harrison succeeded in making an enemy of Jackson, who never forgot an insult.

After two years in Washington, Harrison was ready to return home to his devoted wife and family in Ohio, and he declined to run for another term.

In 1819 he ran for state senator and was elected. Part of his motivation to run may well have been the salary. The building of his 16-room mansion at North Bend had left him nearly broke. He needed money and serving in government was one way to make it. He served one term, then returned home.

In the next few years, Harrison worked hard to gain election to other posts. He announced his candidacy for governor and ran twice for a U.S. Senate seat from Ohio—all without success. Finally, in 1825, he gained election to the Senate and traveled back to Washington. Harrison served on Senate committees that dealt with military affairs and spent much of his time looking

William Henry Harrison in his dress uniform near the end of the War of 1812.

for higher office. He had hoped to be nominated as a candidate for vice president in 1824, but he was not picked. In the election, four major candidates sought the presidency. Andrew Jackson won the most popular and electoral votes, but didn't win a majority in the electoral college. The election was decided in the House of Representatives, which elected John Quincy Adams, the second-place finisher.

Minister to Colombia

In the Senate, Harrison supported the Adams administration and began to campaign for an appointment as ambassador to a foreign country. In 1828, late in Adams's term, he appointed Harrison the first U.S. minister to Colombia, the newly independent country in South America. Apparently, Harrison was content with the appointment, which paid $9,000 a year. He resigned from the Senate and sailed for Colombia.

Just getting to Colombia was a challenge. From New York, Harrison traveled by ship to Venezuela, on the northern coast of South America. From there he traveled overland another 750 miles (1,200 km) on a mule train to Bogotá, the capital of Colombia. He arrived in February 1829, only to learn that Andrew Jackson had defeated Adams in the 1828 election. Harrison knew that Jackson would appoint one of his own supporters as minister of Colombia, so Harrison was out of a job before he had even begun. He served awkwardly as temporary minister while waiting for the new minister to arrive. Although he made friends among the Colombians, he also made enemies by offering advice on matters he knew little about.

The hero of the region was Simón Bolívar, the great liberator who had helped several South American countries gain independence from Spain. Harrison never met Bolívar, who was then in Peru, but he sent him a letter of advice on dealing with the complicated and often dangerous politics of the region. Colombia was one of the most unstable and dangerous places in the Western Hemisphere. In fact, just as Harrison was preparing to leave for home, a revolution against Bolívar broke out in Bogotá. Harrison wasn't able to leave the troubled country until October 1829.

Troubles at Home

All Harrison had to show for his South American junket was a colorful tropical bird he brought home with him. He had no chance of gaining an appointment in Jackson's administration, so he returned to North Bend, where he faced new problems. His son John Cleves Harrison died of typhoid fever, and the Harrisons took in his widow and their six children. In 1832, a flood destroyed the farm's crops. Soon after, Harrison himself became ill. When he recovered,

Simón Bolívar (1783-1830)

Like William Henry Harrison, Simón Bolívar came from a family of great privilege. He was born in Caracas, Venezuela, to wealthy and influential parents. They died when Bolívar was still a child, and he inherited a fortune. He traveled to Europe, and after he returned, he became a political revolutionary, urging the people in Spain's South American colonies to fight for their independence.

Bolívar and other revolutionary leaders captured Caracas in 1810. Over the next 15 years, he liberated Venezuela, Peru, Ecuador, and Colombia from Spanish rule. He created a new country out of northern Peru, which was named Bolivia in his honor.

Bolívar dreamed of a united Spanish America that could become a great nation like the United States. But a lack of cooperation between countries and a growing distrust of Bolívar's own ambitions doomed his dream of unity. After Harrison's departure, Bolívar resigned the presidency of Colombia in 1830 and died soon afterward. Today he is considered one of South America's greatest heroes and is hailed as "the George Washington of South America."

☆ ☆ ☆

he was desperate for money and accepted a position as the clerk of the court of common pleas in nearby Cincinnati.

Meanwhile, the opponents of President Jackson began to organize a new party to fight against his policies and to elect a different president. The group

Simón Bolívar encouraged the peoples of South America to throw off the rule of Spain and become independent nations. Harrison exchanged letters with Bolívar, but the two men never met.

The Whig Party

The Whigs were a major political party from 1834 to the 1850s. In those few years, they elected two presidents and gained strong representation in Congress. They took their name from the Whig party in Great Britain, which had been a major force in the British Parliament since the early 1700s. British Whigs began by opposing the king's party (the Tories). They succeeded over many years in reducing the powers of the monarchy, helping to make Parliament the true governing body of the country.

The "king" the American Whigs opposed was Democratic president Andrew Jackson. Jackson made his reputation by favoring the common people over the rich and privileged—bankers, wealthy merchants, and large landowners. The Whigs believed that he was trying to take power and influence away from traditional leaders of states and communities and might well ruin the country.

The Whigs agreed in opposing Jackson, but they disagreed about many important issues. New England Whigs favored the national bank, which Jackson was driving out of business, but they opposed slavery. Southern Whigs were against the national bank, but believed that their states had a right to keep slavery. Westerners, like Henry Clay, wanted the federal money to develop the west, which other Whigs often opposed. Within twenty years, these disagreements would cause the party to splinter and go out of business.

☆ ☆ ☆

included New England merchants and bankers, westerners who wanted more government spending for roads and other improvements, and southern plantation owners. All these groups saw Jackson's policies and his style of governing as threats to their futures.

The two great leaders of the early Whig Party were senators Henry Clay of Kentucky (above) and Daniel Webster of Massachusetts (next page). Both contributed to the election of Harrison in 1840.

In 1834 these groups formed a new political party—the Whigs. Its leaders included some of the most respected politicians in America: former president John Quincy Adams, and two powerful congressional leaders—Henry Clay of Kentucky and Daniel Webster of Massachusetts. In 1834 Harrison joined the Whig party. It was a move that would greatly improve his political fortunes.

Chapter 4

Tippecanoe and Tyler, Too!

The Election of 1836 ———————

In 1835, William Henry Harrison was 62 years old, a point in life when he might have been considering a quiet retirement. Yet the fires of political ambition still burned in him. He conducted a trial tour of Indiana and Illinois in the summer of 1835 as a presidential candidate, and he gained support both from the public and from influential newspaper editors. As the election of 1836 approached, he was a leading prospect for nomination by the Whig party.

"Some folks are silly enough to have formed a plan to make a president of the United States out of this clerk and clodhopper," Harrison jokingly wrote to his old friend General Solomon Van Rensselaer.

In many ways Harrison was the perfect candidate for the Whigs. He was a military hero like George Washington and Andrew

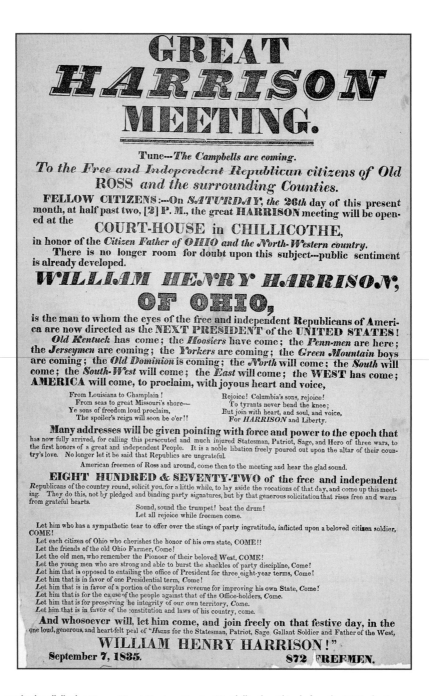

This handbill advertises a "Great Harrison Meeting" in Chillicothe, Ohio, before the 1836 election. The Whigs ran several regional candidates (including Harrison), but Democrat Martin Van Buren won more votes than all the Whigs put together.

Jackson. He was handsome and looked every inch a president. He had an open and appealing manner. Most important of all, he had been away from the national political scene long enough to have no enemies in Washington. His political views on current issues were unknown and could offend no one. He was also a man associated with the west, a part of the country that had captured the national imagination. Such a candidate could seriously increase the appeal of the Whigs, who owed much of their support to wealthy men in the northeast and the south. Whigs in the northwest nominated Harrison and gave him their support.

There were other Whigs who wanted to run, too. Daniel Webster, one of the great orators of the Senate, had the support of his home state of Massachusetts. Democratic senator Hugh L. White from Tennessee had lost the nomination of his party to Vice President Martin Van Buren. His supporters in Tennessee ran him as a "favorite son" with Whig support. So in the end there were three Whig candidates running against the Democrat Van Buren.

Van Buren's campaign stressed that he would carry on the policies of retiring president Andrew Jackson, who remained widely popular among voters. On election day, Van Buren gained more votes than all his Whig opponents together. He was elected president with 170 of the 294 votes in the electoral college. Harrison, however, made a surprisingly good showing. He gained more than

Martin Van Buren (1782-1862)

Martin Van Buren had earned the nickname "the Little Magician" early in his career because of his political skill. But no magic could save him from being a luckless, one-term president. Until his presidency, he seemed the most fortunate of politicians. He had gained almost absolute power in the politics of his home state of New York. He served as senator from New York, governor, then as secretary of state and vice president under Andrew Jackson.

Van Buren was blamed for the economic depression that caused so much suffering during his term. This seems unfair, since his powers as president were limited, and Congress dragged its feet in passing the proposals he did make. In 1837, he called for an independent treasury system to help manage the national money supply, but Congress did not agree to the new treasury system until 1840, three years later. By then, Van Buren was among the most unpopular presidents in history.

Van Buren did achieve some positive things as president, however. He avoided a war with Britain and Canada, despite violent clashes along the U.S.-Canadian border. He also put through the first major legislation for government workers, reducing their workday to ten hours. He ended his term with a national surplus of $1.5 million.

After leaving the presidency, Van Buren tried to gain the Democratic presidential nomination in 1844 and 1848, but he failed both times. In 1848, he ran as the candidate of the Free Soil party, but did not carry a single state. He retired to his estate in Kinderhook, New York, where he died at age 79 on July 24, 1862.

☆ ★ ☆

President Martin Van Buren, who defeated Harrison and the Whigs in 1836. After a disastrous presidency, he lost to Harrison in 1840.

a third of the popular vote and 73 electoral votes, by far the best showing among the Whig candidates.

President Van Buren hoped to continue the successes of the Jackson administration. Even as he took office in March 1837, however, there were signs of trouble. Businesses across the country were failing, and farmers who had borrowed money to buy land couldn't repay their loans. In May, a series of bank failures brought on a nationwide panic, or economic depression. Political and business leaders pleaded with Van Buren to do something to ease the hard times. He called a special session of Congress for September, but by then things were much worse, and Congress refused to enact the program he proposed. The depression eased up briefly during the winter of 1839–40, but the economy continued to suffer through the end of Van Buren's presidential term.

To make matters worse, Van Buren had none of the personal appeal of Andrew Jackson. He was a brilliant politician, but had always worked behind the scenes, directing Jackson's presidential campaigns and serving as a close adviser. Known for his crafty political strategies and his fondness for stylish clothes, Van Buren was an easy target for criticism. It was easy for people to blame him for all the country's troubles, and they did. As the election of 1840 drew near, the Whigs had a real chance to win the presidency.

As in 1836, however, the Whigs were still divided. Henry Clay, who had been a powerful voice in Congress for more than twenty years, was eager to run. So was Daniel Webster of Massachusetts. Yet both men had made many enemies in their years in office. By contrast, Harrison had proved his ability to gain votes, and had said or done nothing since the last election to make enemies. His image as a military hero and a man of the west made him most likely to get elected.

Both Webster and Clay finally conceded the Whig nomination to Harrison, although Clay complained, "I am the most unfortunate man in the history of parties, always run by my friends when sure to be defeated, and now betrayed for a nomination which I, or anyone, would be sure of an election." To gain votes from Whigs in the south, the party nominated John Tyler of Virginia as vice president.

The Whigs did not take winning for granted. Leading Whigs Nicholas Biddle and Thurlow Weed knew the campaign would have to be carefully thought out. The most important thing was not to offend the voters. Harrison's views on political issues were largely unknown, and party leaders decided they should remain so. "Let no Committee, no convention, no town meeting, ever extract from him one single word about what he thinks now or what he will do hereafter," Biddle told his fellow Whigs.

"A Log Cabin and Hard Cider"

Even though he was warned not to say anything controversial, Harrison was encouraged to campaign. In fact, he became the first presidential candidate to campaign actively for himself, setting a new style in presidential politics. His appearances could prove that even at the age of 67 he was still healthy and energetic.

At first, the Democrats did not take Harrison seriously. They attacked him as an ignorant backwoodsman with little ambition. One newspaper editor wrote, "Give him a barrel of hard cider and a pension of two thousand a year and, my word for it, he will sit the remainder of his days in a log cabin."

The author of these words would quickly come to regret them. The Whig campaign leaders turned them into the theme of their campaign. A log cabin and hard cider, a popular and inexpensive alcoholic drink, would become symbols of the simple frontier virtues of William Henry Harrison. Never mind that Harrison had built and lived in mansions in Vincennes and North Bend, or that he had grown up in a fine plantation house in Virginia. As for Harrison's taste in drink, he preferred a good wine to a jug of hard cider. The "man of the people" preferred a quiet evening at home reading the Greek classics to rubbing elbows with backwoodsmen. Still, the "Log Cabin and Hard Cider" theme created huge enthusiasm for Harrison and helped elect him president.

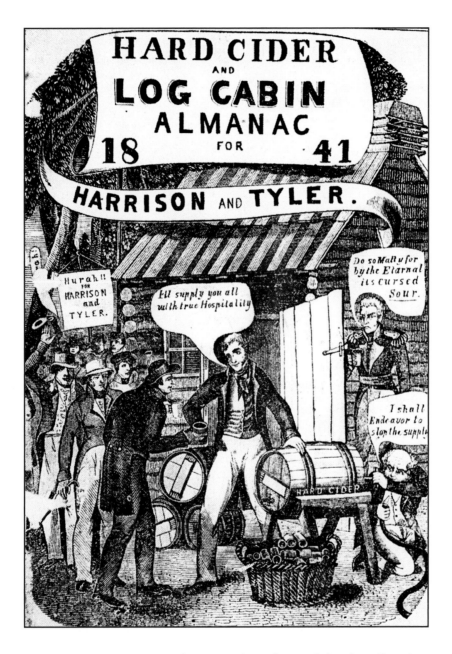

This almanac cover is a campaign piece for Harrison's election, featuring the log cabin and kegs of hard cider. At the right are Harrison's Democratic opponents. Andrew Jackson complains that the cider is "sour," and Martin Van Buren tries to stop the flow of cider from the keg.

The Election Won with Music

Among the most notable features of the election of 1840 was the great number of campaign songs and other music praising one candidate or condemning the other. Never before had music played such a key role in an American political campaign. Dozens of songs were written for the Harrison and Tyler ticket. Perhaps the most famous was "Tip and Ty" that made effective use of the campaign slogan "Tippecanoe and Tyler, Too!" It was written by Alexander Coffman Ross, a jeweler from Zanesville, Ohio. One politician called it "in the political canvas of 1840 what the 'Marseillaise' [now the French national anthem] was to the French Revolution."

Most of these campaign songs were new lyrics written to be sung to old familiar tunes. "The Log Cabin and Hard Cider Candidate," for instance, was set to the tune of "Auld Lang Syne." One verse went,

> Should good old cider be despised,
> And ne'er regarded more?
> Should plain log cabins be despised,
> Our fathers built of yore?
> > For the true old style, my boys!
> > For the true old style,
> > Let's take a mug of cider now,
> > For the true old style.

The Democrats, in contrast, had few campaign songs. Of those, a precious few sang the praises of Martin Van Buren, who did not seem heroic even to his staunchest supporters. Most Democratic songs were attacks on Harrison. This lullaby appeared in a Democratic newspaper and was a reply to "Tip and Ty."

> Hush-a-by-baby,
> Daddy's a Whig,
> Before he comes home
> Hard cider he'll swig.
> Then he'll be tipsy

And over he'll fall,
Down will come daddy,
Tip, Tyler and all.

Another Democratic editorial writer wrote, "Some of the songs I shall never forget. They rang in my ears wherever I went, morning, noon and night. . . . If a Democrat tried to speak, argue, or answer anything that was said or done, he was only saluted with a fresh deluge of music."

Diarist and former New York mayor Philip Hone went so far as to write that Harrison had been "sung into the presidency."

This print showing the log cabin and an American flag also provides the music for the "General Harrison Log Cabin March."

Slogans were another effective part of the campaign. Harrison was often called "Old Tippecanoe," after his victory over the Shawnee in Indiana in 1811. A campaign worker extended the nickname to make a campaign slogan that rolled easily off the tongue: "Tippecanoe and Tyler, Too!" It became one of the most famous campaign slogans in American history.

Parades, Slogans, and Songs

The Whigs' Log Cabin and Hard Cider campaign took the country by storm. Harrison supporters organized torchlight parades in every town and city. Miniature log cabins were pulled on wagons by men or oxen and cider barrels flowed freely for the thirsty public. Sometimes the campaigners dressed up as Indians. The log cabin and the cider keg appeared on everything from handkerchiefs and ribbons to banners and buttons. Harrison rallies were enlivened with such songs as "Log Cabin Candidate" and the "Log Cabin March and Quick Step." There was even a weekly campaign newspaper called the *Log Cabin*, published and edited by a young Whig named Horace Greeley.

Tippecanoe Clubs sprouted up across the nation. Groups of women called "Tippecanoers" prepared feasts while the men built log cabins to be proudly displayed at Whig rallies. Whig orators dramatically described Harrison's victory at Tippecanoe. The battlefield at Tippecanoe, near present-day Lafayette, Indiana,

A cloth handkerchief from 1840 shows the Harrison log cabin against a field of stars.

Horace Greeley was a Whig newspaperman only 29 years old when he supplied many ideas for the Harrison campaign. He thought up the famous campaign slogan "Tippecanoe and Tyler, Too!" and worked tirelessly organizing Whig rallies.

The year after the campaign, Greeley founded the *New York Tribune*, and he became one of the most famous and respected newspaper editors in the United States. After the Whig party dissolved, Greeley joined the new Republican party and helped Abraham Lincoln win the Republican nomination for president in 1860.

Late in his life, Greeley expressed regrets for helping plan a campaign so rich in images and entertainment and so poor in ideas. In 1872, he ran for president himself as a Democrat against the corrupt administration of Republican president Ulysses S. Grant. His campaign slogan "Turn the rascals out!" proved far less effective than "Tippecanoe and Tyler, Too!" He managed to win only six states in the election.

"I have been assailed so bitterly that I hardly know now whether I was running for the presidency or the penitentiary!" Greeley wrote to his daughter. Discouraged and exhausted, Horace Greeley died less than a month after the election.

Horace Greeley was the main inventor of the Log Cabin and Hard Cider campaign that helped elect Harrison. He became a famous newspaper editor and later ran for president himself.

was still a remote location. Yet a rally held there for Harrison and Tyler attracted a reported 60,000 people!

If Harrison was "Old Tip," then his opponent was known as "King Matty," "Martin Van Ruin," and "Van, Van, the used up Man." Van Buren was shown as a sharply dressed aristocrat who dined on French food served on golden plates, while the American people went hungry. In a blistering speech before the House of Representatives, Whig congressman Charles Ogle of Pennsylvania described Van Buren as "strutting by the hour before golden-framed mirrors NINE FEET HIGH and FOUR FEET AND A HALF WIDE in his PALACE as splendid as that of the Caesars, and as richly adorned as the proudest Asiatic mansion."

The Democrats tried to point out that Harrison grew up in the luxury of a Virginia plantation, while Van Buren's father was a tavern keeper in upstate New York. But no one wanted to listen. Image was everything in the presidential election of 1840. Public relations triumphed for the first time in American politics.

Harrison's Victory

The final results of the election were predictable. Harrison trounced Van Buren, winning 234 electoral votes to Van Buren's 60. The popular vote, however, was much closer—about 1,275,000 to 1,125,000, a difference of 150,000. It was the first presidential election in which any candidate received more than a million

"Keep the Ball Rolling!"

The popular phrase "keep the ball rolling" may have originated in the campaign of 1840. During a rally in Baltimore, Maryland, an orator declared that Harrison's campaign was sweeping the country. The next speaker responded by saying, "Well, let's keep the ball rolling!"

One listener in the audience took this advice to heart. He went home and made an enormous ball encased in leather that was ten feet high. Across the ball he wrote the words, "This ball we roll, with all our soul, for Tip and Tyler, too!"

With some help from his fellow townspeople, the man rolled the giant ball to the next town. Soon the fad caught on, and there were giant balls being rolled across every state. One energetic group of Harrison supporters rolled a large paper ball from Kentucky to Baltimore, Maryland, where the National Convention of Whig Young Men was being held.

Today we still say "keep the ball rolling" when we want someone's success to continue.

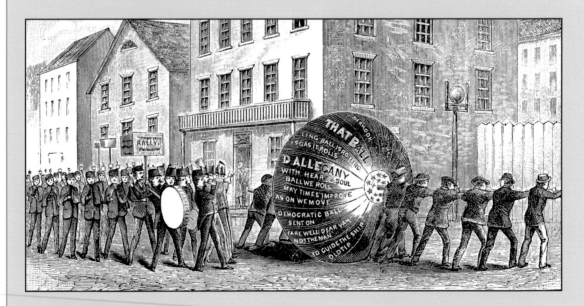

Many Harrison parades featured huge balls that were rolled from town to town. One of the campaign slogans was "Keep the Ball Rolling!"

votes. The Whig campaign was so successful that many Whig candidates for Congress were swept into office. The Whigs won control of both the U.S. Senate and the House of Representatives.

Harrison, who honestly thought he could unite the country and provide the leadership America needed, was delighted with his victory. But his wife had misgivings, saying, "I wish that my husband's friends had left him where he is, happy and contented in retirement." Her words would soon prove grimly prophetic.

Chapter 5

The President-Elect in Washington ——

President-elect Harrison was in no hurry to get to Washington after his election. He paid a visit to Kentucky, home of his rival Henry Clay. From there he returned to Cincinnati, his home base, and resigned from his job as clerk of the court. On January 26, 1841, he left the city on the steamboat *Ben Franklin*. "Gentleman and fellow-citizens," he said, addressing the crowd gathered to see him off, "perhaps this may be the last time I may have the pleasure of speaking to you on earth or seeing you. I . . . bid you farewell."

Mrs. Harrison had been too ill to make the trip to Washington and was to come along in the spring when the weather was warmer. In the meantime, Harrison's widowed daughter-in-law Jane Irwin Harrison would serve as the White House hostess.

Harrison traveled to Pittsburgh, then to Baltimore, and finally arrived in the capital on February 9, his 68th birthday. It was snowing, but Harrison refused an umbrella and walked to the City Hall. Perhaps he wanted to show everyone he was as fit and ready for the job as any younger man.

He also wanted to show he was a graceful winner. He called on Martin Van Buren at the White House, the first time an incoming president had ever visited an outgoing president. The meeting was cordial and lasted half an hour. Van Buren genuinely liked Harrison and invited him back to dinner a few days later.

Although he found Harrison warm and generous, Van Buren was perplexed at his attitude toward his new position. "He does not seem to realize the vast importance of his elevation. . . ." Van Buren said. "He is as tickled with the presidency as is a young woman with a new bonnet."

Harrison was making serious preparations, however. He chose Daniel Webster as his secretary of state and picked other able men for his cabinet. Henry Clay refused an appointment. He preferred to remain in the Senate, where he could manage the Whigs in Congess and help pass the party's legislative program. Clay expected that Harrison would follow his advice and would sign into law any bill passed by the Whigs.

William Henry Harrison, ninth president of the United States.

Inauguration Day

Inauguration Day, March 4, 1841, was miserable. It was cold and rainy with a chilling wind. Yet the weather did not dampen the spirits of those present. Harrison rode down Pennsylvania Avenue on his favorite horse, Old Whitey. The crowds were noisy and enthusiastic, continuing the festive mood of the most

Presidential Inaugurations

The inauguration of President Harrison was one of the most elaborate up to that time, but each presidential inauguration brought some new tradition to that celebrated ceremony.

The first two presidential inaugurations of George Washington were not held in Washington, but in New York and Philadelphia, the first two national capitals. After the oath was given at his first inaugural, Washington said spontaneously, "So help me God." Every president since has followed likewise.

John Adams, the second U.S. president, was the first to receive the oath from the Chief Justice of the United States. Thomas Jefferson started the tradition of writing to Congress for formal acceptance of the inauguration and its time. At Martin Van Buren's inauguration the outgoing president, Andrew Jackson, rode to the Capitol in a carriage with the incoming president for the first time.

William Henry Harrison's inauguration marked several firsts. He was the first president-elect to arrive in Washington for his swearing in by railroad. The first official parade followed his inauguration at the Capitol. Harrison's address, at 10,000 words, set a record for length. In contrast, George Washington's second inaugural address was all of 135 words, the shortest on record.

☆☆☆

Huge crowds came to Washington on March 4, 1841, to celebrate Harrison's inauguration as president.

colorful presidential campaign in history. According to former president John Quincy Adams, the crowds gave Harrison "demonstrations of popular feeling unexampled since that of Washington in 1789."

Harrison appeared on the steps of the Capitol bareheaded and without an overcoat. Then he proceeded to give the longest inaugural address in history. It ran nearly 10,000 words, and took Harrison an hour and forty minutes to deliver. "Old Tip took a long time to say very little," reported Daniel Webster, who had edited an even longer draft of the speech to shorten it.

One of the main concerns of the Whigs was to reduce presidential power after the excesses of Andrew Jackson. Harrison promised in his address to reduce the role of the president. He promised to serve only one term and called for a constitutional amendment to limit future presidents to a single term.

In a period when disagreements between North and South were becoming more and more worrisome, Harrison stressed the importance of maintaining the union of all the states. "Of all the great interests which appertain to our country, that of union—cordial, confiding, fraternal union—is by far the most important, since it is the only true and sure guaranty of all others," the president said.

If the Union was to be preserved, there would have to be some new compromise on slavery. Harrison declared his view that Congress did not have the

The States During the Presidency of William Henry Harrison

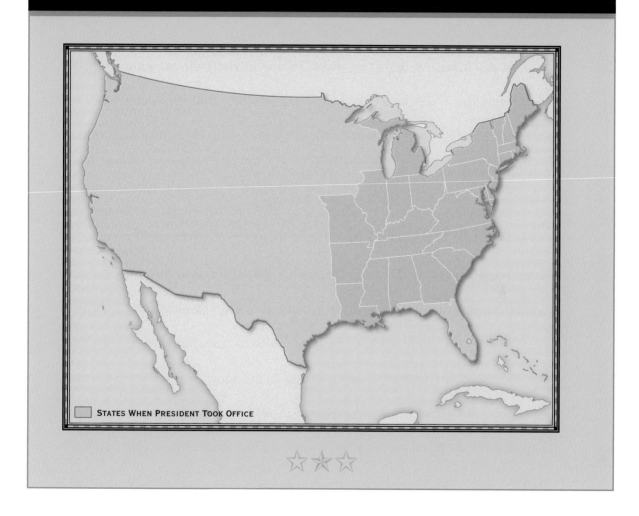

STATES WHEN PRESIDENT TOOK OFFICE

★★★

power to abolish slavery in Washington, D.C., which pleased his southern supporters. He pleased westerners by pledging to establish free land grants in the territories. He also spoke for his old comrades in the military, favoring pensions for soldiers and sailors who had served the United States.

At the inaugural balls that night, President Harrison continued to show amazing stamina. One guest called him "the indefatigable President [who] for hours made the rounds of a hundred little circles, all so many eddies of delight in which he sported unrestrained."

Difficult First Days

The first few weeks of the president's administration were not happy ones. On his first days in the White House, Harrison was overwhelmed by office seekers—men who were seeking appointments to government jobs. He had stated firmly in his inaugural address that the *"spoils" system* of political patronage used by Jackson and Van Buren would not be followed in his presidency. However, Harrison was by nature a kind man who wanted to help whomever he could. In addition, the Whigs had never controlled the national government before, and there were hundreds of party supporters who believed they deserved consideration.

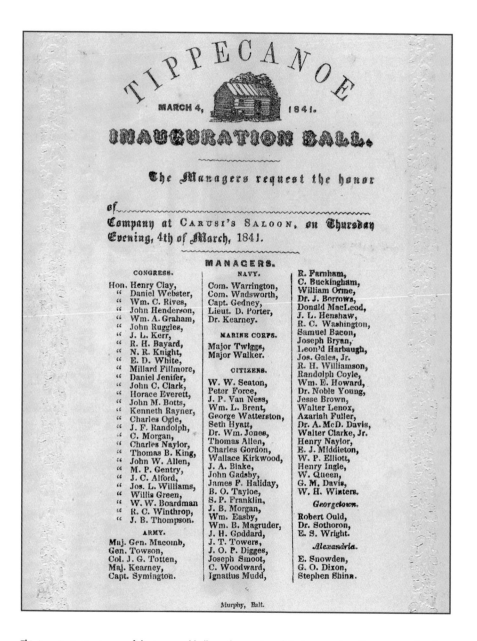

This is an invitation to one of the inaugural balls on the evening of the inauguration. Harrison visited each party and stayed until late in the evening.

Presidential Peril: The Spoils System

Under the "spoils" system, public offices and government jobs were given as political rewards for loyal party service. Martin Van Buren had developed a "political machine" using the system in New York State, and he helped establish it in the federal government under Andrew Jackson. The system got its name from New York senator William L. Marcy, who explained that in politics as in war, "to the victor belongs the spoils."

From the time Harrison arrived in Washington in February, hundreds of Whig office seekers, including many of his old friends and supporters, came to see him personally about appointments. They brought letters outlining their qualifications and connections and more letters of recommendation from others. One day Harrison greeted an old friend from Cincinnati with relief. "I am glad with all my heart to see you for I know that you do not want an office," he said.

After the inauguration, a crowd of office seekers even interrupted a cabinet meeting and refused to leave unless Harrison "would *then* receive their papers and pledge himself to attend them." The president agreed, and when the group left, his pockets, hat, and arms were overflowing with bundles of letters.

The winning political party still has the right to appoint its faithful members to the highest offices in government. For thousands of lesser positions, applicants now take civil service examinations and cannot be thrown out of their jobs when a different political party takes power.

☆ ☆ ☆

However healthy Harrison seemed to be, the long campaign, the victory trip to Washington, and the inauguration left him with limited energy. He missed his wife and children and the support and comfort they could have offered him. Through the early days of his administration, he concentrated on making political appointments. However, it dawned slowly on Harrison that the job of president was much bigger than he had imagined. Leaders of federal agencies wanted decisions made; congessmen wanted support for legislation; local Whig leaders wanted to meet him. Foreign nations wanted attention, too.

A week after he took office, an international crisis arose. During Van Buren's administration, a group of Canadians began a revolt against the rule of Britain. Some Americans tried to bring supplies to the rebels on the Niagara River, part of the border between Canada and the United States. Canadian loyalists set fire to their ship, the *Caroline*, and let it drift downstream over Niagara Falls. Now police in Buffalo, New York, arrested a Canadian who had helped burn the *Caroline* and had killed an American. The British government demanded the release of the Canadian and threatened to go to war if he was not let go. Harrison sent Attorney General John Crittenden to New York to discuss the issue with Governor William Seward. Seward pardoned the Canadian, and later Secretary of State Webster negotiated a treaty with Great Britain.

Canadian officials seized the *Caroline*, a U.S. ship, on the Niagara River in 1837 because it was supporting a rebellion against the Canadian government. They set the ship afire, and let it drift over Niagara Falls. When one official was arrested in the United States in 1841, Canada and Britain demanded his release and threatened war. Harrison's government arranged for the man's release.

A Fatal Illness

Oddly, Harrison took great pleasure in small household errands. While Clay and Webster ran his administration, he would walk out early in the morning to buy food for the White House kitchen. On the morning of March 27, 1841, a rain shower interrupted his walk. Instead of going home to dry off, Harrison went on to the home of a military officer to offer him a diplomatic post. After his long trudge through the icy slush, Harrison caught a chill. That evening after dinner, he sent for a physician. The physician concluded that he had pneumonia.

Pneumonia—the Deadly Disease

If President Harrison were living today, he might have survived his brief bout with pneumonia. Antibiotics discovered in the 1940s would likely have saved his life. In 1841, however, pneumonia was often fatal, killing more than 30 percent of the people who got it. Today, thanks to modern medicine, that number has been reduced to 5 percent.

The physicians who attended Harrison in his last days had few tools to fight the disease. The pills, drugs, salves, and powders that they used were little help. A patient had to rely on his or her own natural defenses to recover. Pneumonia was especially dangerous for the youngest and the oldest in the population.

While Harrison's death was saddening to all, most people at the time probably considered him lucky to have lived to the age of 68. A child born in the 1840s had an average life expectancy of only 40 years.

☆★☆

Harrison remained in bed for a week and started to feel better, but then he relapsed and was sicker than ever. While his doctors tried to be optimistic, Harrison knew he was a dying man. "Ah, Fanny," he confided to one of his female attendants, "I am ill, very ill, much more so than they think me."

Soon the doctors reached the grim conclusion that Harrison was dying. The future of the nation he had been chosen to govern was still very much on the dying president's mind. "Sir, I wish you to understand the true principles of the government," he said to one of his doctors. "I wish them carried out. I ask nothing more." They were his last recorded words.

Harrison lies near death at the White House less than a month after he took office.

William Henry Harrison died at 12:30 A.M. on April 4, 1841. He had been in office a few hours less than one month. His presidency remains the shortest in American history.

A Presidential Funeral

When people learned of Harrison's death, they were stunned. Throughout the colorful campaign, they had grown close to "Old Tip," the soldier-politician, and now they genuinely mourned his passing. Government leaders were faced with a new situation. Harrison was the first president to die in office, and there were no *precedents* to follow.

The first question was the funeral. The planners studied funerals for monarchs and heads of state in Europe. The dead president was laid in a mahogany coffin in the East Room of the White House. The coffin had a glass in the lid to allow mourners to see his face. The funeral was a grand but solemn affair. The coffin sat atop a funeral car on a wagon draped in black velvet. The wagon was pulled by white horses along Pennsylvania Avenue. The Marine Band followed behind the coffin playing "President Harrison's Funeral Dirge" and other mournful pieces. Harrison had been sung into the White House, and now music would accompany his final departure from it. His horse, Old Whitey, who had carried him to the inaugural only a month earlier, now walked riderless in his funeral procession.

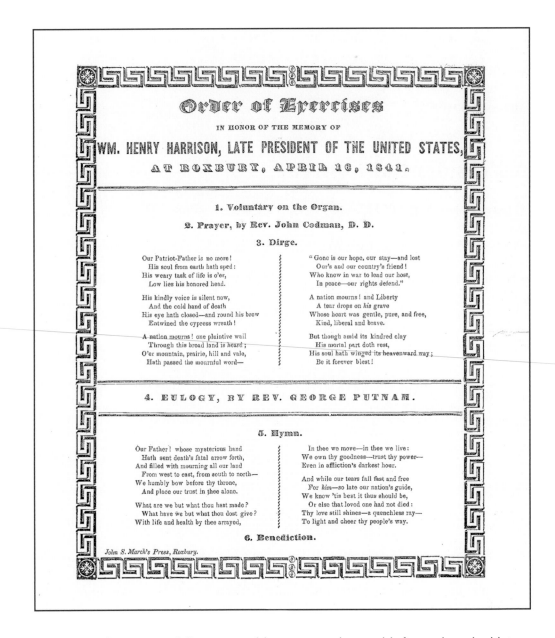

Memorial services for Harrison were held in towns around the country as people mourned the first president to die while in office. This service took place in Roxbury, Massachusetts.

Harrison's body was placed with full honors in a vault in the congressional cemetery. Two months later, Mrs. Harrison had her husband's body removed to the family tomb in North Bend, the ninth president's final resting place.

Chapter 6

What Kind of President? ————————

What kind of president would William Henry Harrison have been if he had lived through his term? Based on his short record in the White House, he would not have been a strong president. He said in his inaugural address that he would play down the importance of the president and limit his own role. In addition, powerful Whig leaders, including Clay and Webster, expected Harrison to be a figurehead president while they determined the government's actions.

Strengths and Weaknesses ————————

Still, there were qualities of leadership that Harrison shared with Jackson and that other great military leader and president, George Washington. He was devoted to the Union, affable, and personally charming; he had an impressive military record that earned him the

A campaign poster for Harrison, reminding people of his career as a military leader.

★ LEGACY ★

respect of the people and the devotion of the soldiers who served under him. If Harrison had been elected president ten or twenty years earlier, he might have demonstrated the strong leadership that the country needed. His advanced age and limited stamina did not make him good presidential material in 1840.

Before he contracted the pneumonia that killed him, Harrison seemed overwhelmed and bewildered by the deluge of office seekers who dogged his steps. For the most part, he seemed willing to let Webster and Clay run the affairs of state. Yet there were a few signs that he might have taken a stronger hand.

Henry Clay arrived in Washington expecting to dominate the new president completely. In a meeting before the inauguration, Clay presented a list of his friends and supporters to be appointed to positions in the administration. Harrison reminded him that the Whig campaign had promised to end the "spoils" system and refused to approve all of Clay's requests. Harrison then sent Clay a note saying, "You are too impetuous." Clay was outraged and returned to Kentucky, never to see Harrison alive again.

A New Kind of Campaign

The famous campaign that elected Harrison is perhaps the central legacy of his brief presidency. The Log Cabin and Hard Cider campaign was the first modern American political campaign and served as a model for many presidential campaigns to come. For the first time the presentation or "packaging" of the candidate for president was more important than what skills the candidate had or what he stood for. Whig leaders used slogans, campaign songs, special events, parades, newspapers, pamphlets, and almanacs to create an image that could be "sold" to the public. Torchlight parades, little log cabins, and barrels of free cider were not only fun, but created an image of Harrison as a man of the people, that in many ways the real Harrison was not. The campaign was a great success, but perhaps was not the best way to choose a president.

The campaign did have its good side, however. It got thousands of people involved in politics, including women, who could not vote. It also brought out more voters than had ever participated in a presidential election. Many of those who helped elect Harrison continued to be involved in politics in later years as the nation debated the difficult issues of slavery, states rights, and the Union.

Establishing a Precedent

Another important legacy of the Harrison presidency is that it set a precedent for the transfer of power. When Harrison died, the Constitution was clear that the vice president would succeed to the office, but it was less clear what powers the new president should have. Some politicians at the time insisted that the new president, John Tyler, should be merely a caretaker, holding down the office until

A ribbon worn by campaigners for Harrison with the heading
"Our Country's Hope."

the next election. Tyler, however, believed that he should have the same powers that Harrison would have had, and he refused to act simply as a caretaker. He used all the powers of the presidency, including his veto, taking full responsibility as president in his own right. As it turned out, he was not a successful president, but his determination to use the full powers of the office set an important precedent.

Vice President John Tyler receives the news that President Harrison has died.

John Tyler (1790–1862)

Vice President John Tyler was at home in Williamsburg, Virginia, when he received the news of Harrison's death. A vice president had few responsibilities at the time, and he was not required to be in Washington when Congress was not in session. He hadn't even been informed that the president was ill.

Tyler served as president all but one month of Harrison's term of office.

A Virginia lawyer who served as his state's governor and senator, Tyler was a former Democrat who had switched to the Whig party to oppose Andrew Jackson. He was chosen as Harrison's running mate for his potential to get southern votes for the ticket. He proved not to agree with most Whigs on important issues. Before his term was up, his cabinet had resigned and the Whigs had thrown him out of the party. When the next election came, neither Whigs nor Democrats considered him for the nomination, and he retired from politics.

Tyler managed to do a few notable things as president, among them assuring the annexation of Texas by the United States. But he is also remembered as the first president to be married while in office. His first wife died in the White House after a long illness. His second marriage, to the young, vivacious Julia Gardiner, was the talk of Washington. Together they had seven children, which, when added to the eight children Tyler had with his first wife, makes him the president with the most offspring.

☆☆☆

Since Tyler, seven other vice presidents have taken office when a president died or resigned, and they too have become full independent presidents, not caretakers. Several ran for president at the end of their terms and were elected to full terms of office.

In the last analysis, William Henry Harrison is a minor figure among American presidents. He was a soldier whose military victories were somewhat inflated and a president who didn't live long enough to leave his stamp on the office. Perhaps Harrison should best be remembered for two things—for helping establish the first "American West" in the Northwest Territory and for being the only president to have a grandson who also rose to the highest office—Benjamin Harrison, the 23rd president of the United States.

Birth:	February 9, 1773
Birthplace:	Berkeley Plantation in Charles City County, Virginia
Parents:	Benjamin Harrison V and Elizabeth Bassett Harrison
Brothers & Sisters:	All older: Elizabeth (b. 1751), Anne (b. 1753), Benjamin (b. 1755), Lucy (b. about 1760?), Carter (b. about 1765?), Sarah (b. 1770)
Education:	Hampden-Sydney College, Virginia, the Medical School of Pennsylvania in Philadelphia
Occupation:	Military officer, public official
Marriage:	To Anna Tuthill Symmes on November 25, 1795
Children:	(See "First Lady First Facts" at right)
Political Parties:	Democratic-Republican; Whig (as president)
Public Offices:	1798–99 Secretary of the Northwest Territory
	1799–00 Territorial Delegate to U.S. Congress
	1800–12 Governor of the Indiana Territory
	1812–14 Commander of Armies in the Northwest
	1816–19 Member, U.S. House of Representatives from Ohio
	1819–21 State Senator, Ohio Senate
	1825–28 U.S. Senator from Ohio
	1828–29 U.S. Minister to Colombia
	1841 Ninth President of the United States
His Vice President:	John Tyler, who succeeded to the presidency when Harrison died, serving as the tenth president from April 1841 to March 1845
Major Actions as President:	None
Firsts:	Longest inaugural address before or since (1 hour 40 minutes)
	First president to die while in office
Death:	April 4, 1841, in the White House, Washington, D.C.
Age at Death:	68 years
Burial Place:	North Bend, Ohio

Fast Facts

Anna Tuthill Symmes Harrison

Born:	July 25, 1775
Birthplace:	Flatbrook, New Jersey
Parents:	John Cleves Symmes and Mrs. Tuthill Symmes
Education:	An academy in Easthampton, Long Island; private school in New York
Marriage:	To William Henry Harrison on November 25, 1795
Children:	Elizabeth Bassett Harrison (1796–1846)
	John Cleves Symmes Harrison (1798–1830)
	Lucy Singleton Harrison (1800–1826)
	William Henry Harrison (1802–1838)
	John Scott Harrison (1804–1878)
	Benjamin Harrison (1806–1840)
	Mary Symmes Harrison (1809–1842)
	Carter Bassett Harrison (1811–1839)
	Anna Tuthill Harrison (1813–1865)
	James Findlay Harrison (1814–1817)
Died:	February 25, 1864
Age at Death:	88 years
Burial Place:	North Bend, Ohio

Timeline

1773	1775	1776	1783	1787
William Henry Harrison is born on February 9	The Revolutionary War begins at Lexington and Concord, Massachusetts	Benjamin Harrison V, William Henry's father, is a signer of the Declaration of Independence	The Revolutionary War ends in independence for the American colonies	Harrison attends Hampden-Sydney College; the U.S. Constitution is framed in Philadelphia

1798	1800	1809	1810	1811
Appointed secretary of the Northwest Territory by President John Adams	The Northwest Territory is divided in two; Harrison is appointed governor of the Indiana Territory, the westernmost half, by President John Adams	Negotiates the Treaty of Fort Wayne, gaining land concessions from Native Americans	Meets with Shawnee chief Tecumseh at Vincennes	Defeats the Shawnees at the Battle of Tippecanoe on November 7

1819	1822	1825	1828	1829
Elected to the state senate of Ohio	Loses a close race for a U.S. Senate seat in Ohio	Elected to the U.S. Senate	Appointed first U.S. minister to Colombia by President John Quincy Adams	Returns from Colombia

1789	1790	1791	1792	1795
George Washington is chosen the first president of the United States	Harrison studies medicine in Philadelphia with Dr. Benjamin Rush	Harrison's father dies on April 25; Harrison becomes an ensign in the U.S. Army and travels to Fort Pitt	General Wayne takes charge of forces in the Northwest Territory	Harrison fights in the Battle of Fallen Timbers against the Shawnee and Miami; marries Anna Symmes on November 25

1812	1813	1814	1815	1816
Appointed brigadier general, commanding the Northwest armies in the War of 1812; resigns as governor of Indiana Territory	Defeats the British and Indians at the Battle of the Thames River on October 5	Resigns from the army, returns with his family to North Bend, Ohio	General Andrew Jackson defeats the British at the Battle of New Orleans	Harrison is elected to the House of Representatives from Ohio and serves one term

1834	1836	1840	1841
Joins the Whig Party	Runs as one of three Whig candidates for president; places second to Democrat Martin Van Buren, who becomes president	Harrison is nominated for president by the Whigs; after Tippecanoe and Tyler, Too! campaign, he is elected ninth president	Inaugurated on March 4; dies April 4 at 12:30 a.m.

Glossary

aide-de-camp: a confidential assistant to a military officer

bill: a draft of a new law to be considered and voted on by Congress

electoral vote: in U.S. presidential elections, the votes cast by members of the electoral college, who gather according to the Constitution to cast votes for presidential candidates based on votes cast by citizens in their state (*see also* **popular vote**)

impress: in naval history, to take seamen captive (often from an enemy ship) and force them to work as crewmen against their will

pneumonia: an illness (usually caused by bacteria or a virus) that causes inflammation of the lungs; until the mid-1900s, it was fatal in about one-third of all cases

popular vote: in U.S. elections, the tally of votes cast by individuals in the election (*see also* **electoral vote**)

precedent: an action that becomes a model for the action of others in similar circumstances in the future

"spoils" system: a political group's plan to gain power and influence by awarding government jobs and contracts to faithful party members

Further Reading

★ ★ ★ ★ ★

Archer, Jules. *Winners and Losers: How Elections Work in America.* New York: Harcourt Brace Jovanovich, 1984.

Blassingame, Wyatt. *The Look-It-Up Book of Presidents.* New York: Random House, 1993.

Brandt, Nat. "The Harrison Bandwagon." *American Heritage,* October 1975, pp. 18–27.

Durant, John, and Alice Durant. *Pictorial History of American Presidents.* New York: A. S. Barnes and Company, 1955.

Silber, Irwin. *Songs America Voted By.* Harrisburg, PA: Stackpole Books, 1971.

Stefoff, Rebecca. *William Henry Harrison, Ninth President of the United States.* Ada, OK: Garrett Educational Corporation, 1990.

Whitney, David C. *The American Presidents: Biographies of the Chief Executives from Washington To Bush.* Pleasantville, NY: Reader's Digest Association, 1993.

Young, Stanley. *Tippecanoe and Tyler, Too! The Story of William Henry Harrison.* Landmark Book Series. New York: Random House, 1957.

MORE ADVANCED READING

Cleaves, Freeman. *Old Tippecanoe: William Henry Harrison and His Time.* American Political Biographical Press, 1990.

Hall, James N. *Memoir of the Public Service of William Henry Harrison.* Manchester, NH: Ayer Company Publishers, 1972.

Harrison, William Henry. *Mid-American Frontier: Messages and Letters of William Henry Harrison 1812–1816.* Manchester, NH: Ayer Company Publishers, 1975.

Huston, James. *Counterpoint: Tecumseh and William Henry Harrison.* Lawrenceville, VA: Brunswick Publishing Company, 1987.

Peterson, Norma Lois. *Presidencies of William Henry Harrison and John Tyler.* American Presidency Series. Lawrence: University Press of Kansas, 1982.

Places to Visit

Berkeley Plantation

12602 Harrison Landing Road

Charles City, Virginia 23030

(804) 829-6018

The birthplace of William Henry Harrison on the James River between Richmond and Williamsburg, Virginia.

Harrison Mansion (Grouseland)

3 West Scott Street

Vincennes, Indiana 47591

(812) 882-2096

The home Harrison built for his family in Vincennes (in present-day Indiana) while serving as governor of the Indiana Territory. The family lived there from 1803 to 1812.

Tippecanoe Battlefield

Off State Route 43, 1.2 miles south of I-65

Battle Ground, Indiana 47920

(765) 567-2147

The site on the Tippecanoe River where Harrison first won fame as a military commander. It is just north of Lafayette, Indiana, about 140 miles (225 km) north-northeast of Vincennes.

Harrison Tomb State Memorial

Cliff Road, west off U.S. Route 50

North Bend, Ohio 45052

(614) 297-2630 or 1-800-686-1535

Harrison's impressive tomb and memorial is located near the family's longtime home in North Bend, Ohio, about 15 miles (24 km) west of Cincinnati.

Indiana Historical Society

450 West Ohio Street

Indianapolis, Indiana 46202

(317) 232-1882

The Historical Society holds many important documents on the early history of the Indiana Territory during Harrison's years as governor.

The White House

1600 Pennsylvania Avenue NW

Washington, D.C. 20500

Visitors' Office: (202) 456-7041

Harrison died in the White House after living there for less than a month.

Online Sites of Interest

⭐ **Internet Public Library, Presidents of the United States (IPL POTUS)**

http://www.ipl.org/ref/POTUS/whharrison.html

This site includes concise information about Harrison and his presidency and links to other useful sites.

⭐ **Presidential Biographies**

http://www.americanpresident.org/

Detailed and informative biographies of the presidents, providing background information on their early lives, political careers, families, and more.

⭐ **Presidential Inaugural Addresses**

http://www.bartleby.com/124/pres26.html

Harrison's complete inaugural address, the longest in presidential history, is here as well as access to the inaugural address of every other president.

⭐ **The White House**

http://www.whitehouse.gov

Information about the current president and vice president; White House history and tours; biographies of past presidents and their families; a virtual tour of the historic building, current events, trivia quizzes, and much more.

⭐ **Indiana Historical Bureau**

http://www.statelib.lib.in.us/www/ihb/ihb.htm

Contains a portrait of Harrison as Indiana governor and a brief biography. There is much more information about Indiana's early history during Harrison's time on this site.

Table of Presidents

	1. George Washington	2. John Adams	3. Thomas Jefferson	4. James Madison
Took office	Apr 30 1789	Mar 4 1797	Mar 4 1801	Mar 4 1809
Left office	Mar 3 1797	Mar 3 1801	Mar 3 1809	Mar 3 1817
Birthplace	Westmoreland Co, VA	Braintree, MA	Shadwell, VA	Port Conway, VA
Birth date	Feb 22 1732	Oct 20 1735	Apr 13 1743	Mar 16 1751
Death date	Dec 14 1799	July 4 1826	July 4 1826	June 28 1836

	9. William H. Harrison	10. John Tyler	11. James K. Polk	12. Zachary Taylor
Took office	Mar 4 1841	Apr 6 1841	Mar 4 1845	Mar 5 1849
Left office	Apr 4 1841•	Mar 3 1845	Mar 3 1849	July 9 1850•
Birthplace	Berkeley, VA	Greenway, VA	Mecklenburg Co, NC	Barboursville, VA
Birth date	Feb 9 1773	Mar 29 1790	Nov 2 1795	Nov 24 1784
Death date	Apr 4 1841	Jan 18 1862	June 15 1849	July 9 1850

	17. Andrew Johnson	18. Ulysses S. Grant	19. Rutherford B. Hayes	20. James A. Garfield
Took office	Apr 15 1865	Mar 4 1869	Mar 4 1877	Mar 4 1881
Left office	Mar 3 1869	Mar 3 1877	Mar 3 1881	Sept 19 1881•
Birthplace	Raleigh, NC	Point Pleasant, OH	Delaware, OH	Orange, OH
Birth date	Dec 29 1808	Apr 27 1822	Oct 4 1822	Nov 19 1831
Death date	July 31 1875	July 23 1885	Jan 17 1893	Sept 19 1881

5. James Monroe	6. John Quincy Adams	7. Andrew Jackson	8. Martin Van Buren
Mar 4 1817	Mar 4 1825	Mar 4 1829	Mar 4 1837
Mar 3 1825	Mar 3 1829	Mar 3 1837	Mar 3 1841
Westmoreland Co, VA	Braintree, MA	The Waxhaws, SC	Kinderhook, NY
Apr 28 1758	July 11 1767	Mar 15 1767	Dec 5 1782
July 4 1831	Feb 23 1848	June 8 1845	July 24 1862

13. Millard Fillmore	14. Franklin Pierce	15. James Buchanan	16. Abraham Lincoln
July 9 1850	Mar 4 1853	Mar 4 1857	Mar 4 1861
Mar 3 1853	Mar 3 1857	Mar 3 1861	Apr 15 1865•
Locke Township, NY	Hillsborough, NH	Cove Gap, PA	Hardin Co, KY
Jan 7 1800	Nov 23 1804	Apr 23 1791	Feb 12 1809
Mar 8 1874	Oct 8 1869	June 1 1868	Apr 15 1865

21. Chester A. Arthur	22. Grover Cleveland	23. Benjamin Harrison	24. Grover Cleveland
Sept 19 1881	Mar 4 1885	Mar 4 1889	Mar 4 1893
Mar 3 1885	Mar 3 1889	Mar 3 1893	Mar 3 1897
Fairfield, VT	Caldwell, NJ	North Bend, OH	Caldwell, NJ
Oct 5 1830	Mar 18 1837	Aug 20 1833	Mar 18 1837
Nov 18 1886	June 24 1908	Mar 13 1901	June 24 1908

	25. William McKinley	26. Theodore Roosevelt	27. William H. Taft	28. Woodrow Wilson
Took office	Mar 4 1897	Sept 14 1901	Mar 4 1909	Mar 4 1913
Left office	Sept 14 1901•	Mar 3 1909	Mar 3 1913	Mar 3 1921
Birthplace	Niles, OH	New York, NY	Cincinnati, OH	Staunton, VA
Birth date	Jan 29 1843	Oct 27 1858	Sept 15 1857	Dec 28 1856
Death date	Sept 14 1901	Jan 6 1919	Mar 8 1930	Feb 3 1924

	33. Harry S. Truman	34. Dwight D. Eisenhower	35. John F. Kennedy	36. Lyndon B. Johnson
Took office	Apr 12 1945	Jan 20 1953	Jan 20 1961	Nov 22 1963
Left office	Jan 20 1953	Jan 20 1961	Nov 22 1963•	Jan 20 1969
Birthplace	Lamar, MO	Denison, TX	Brookline, MA	Johnson City, TX
Birth date	May 8 1884	Oct 14 1890	May 29 1917	Aug 27 1908
Death date	Dec 26 1972	Mar 28 1969	Nov 22 1963	Jan 22 1973

	41. George Bush	42. Bill Clinton	43. George W. Bush	
Took office	Jan 20 1989	Jan 20 1993	Jan 20 2001	
Left office	Jan 20 1993	Jan 20 2001	—	
Birthplace	Milton, MA	Hope, AR	New Haven, CT	
Birth date	June 12 1924	Aug 19 1946	July 6 1946	
Death date	—	—	—	

29. Warren G. Harding	**30. Calvin Coolidge**	**31. Herbert Hoover**	**32. Franklin D. Roosevelt**
Mar 4 1921	Aug 2 1923	Mar 4 1929	Mar 4 1933
Aug 2 1923•	Mar 3 1929	Mar 3 1933	**Apr 12 1945•**
Blooming Grove, OH	Plymouth, VT	West Branch, IA	Hyde Park, NY
Nov 21 1865	July 4 1872	Aug 10 1874	Jan 30 1882
Aug 2 1923	Jan 5 1933	Oct 20 1964	Apr 12 1945

37. Richard M. Nixon	**38. Gerald R. Ford**	**39. Jimmy Carter**	**40. Ronald Reagan**
Jan 20 1969	Aug 9 1974	Jan 20 1977	Jan 20 1981
Aug 9 1974★	Jan 20 1977	Jan 20 1981	Jan 20 1989
Yorba Linda, CA	Omaha, NE	Plains, GA	Tampico, IL
Jan 9 1913	July 14 1913	Oct 1 1924	Feb 11 1911
Apr 22 1994	—	—	—

• Indicates the president died while in office.

★ Richard Nixon resigned before his term expired.

Index

Page numbers in *italics* indicate illustrations.

About the Author

Steven Otfinoski attended Boston University and graduated with a B.A. from Antioch College in Yellow Springs, Ohio. He has written more than a hundred books for young adults and children. Although this is his first biography of a U.S. president, he has written biographies of such world leaders as Nelson Mandela, Mikhail Gorbachev, and Boris Yeltsin. Among his more recent books are *African Americans in the Performing Arts*; *Bugsy Siegel and the Postwar Boom*; *John Wilkes Booth and the Civil War*; *Marco Polo: To China and Back*; *Francisco Coronado: In Search of the Seven Cities of Gold*; *Nations In Transitions: Afghanistan*; *It's My State! Maryland*; *Celebrate the States: Georgia*; and *Whodunit: Science Solves the Crime*. He has also written two books on popular music for adults—*The Golden Age of Rock Instrumentals* and *The Golden Age of Novelty Songs*.

Mr. Otfinoski lives in Connecticut with his wife Beverly, an editor and teacher, and their two children Daniel and Martha. Among his hobbies are reading, listening to and collecting rock music of the 1950s and 1960s, and playing tennis.